SON • OF • A • MEECH

971   Donato, Andy, 1937-   07967
.0647   Son of a Meech : political cartoons / Andy Donato. -
0207   - Toronto : Key Porter Books, c1990.
Don   1 v. (unpaged) : ill.

        0440873X   ISBN:1550132679 (pbk.)

        1. Mulroney, Brian, 1939- - Caricatures and cartoons.
        2. Canada - Politics and government - 1984- -
        Caricatures and cartoons. I. Title

5459   90OCT09   06/ex   1-00954942

ANDY DONATO

SON • OF • A • MEECH

POLITICAL CARTOONS

KEY PORTER BOOKS

Canadian Cataloguing in Publication Data

Donato, Andy, 1937–
  Son of a Meech

ISBN 1-55013-267-9

1. Canada – Politics and government – 1984–   .
Caricatures and cartoons.*   2. Canadian wit and
humor, Pictorial.   I. Title.

NC1449.D65A4 1990   971.064′7′0207   C90-094874-4

Typesetting: Q Composition Inc.
Printed and bound in Canada

Key Porter Books Limited
70 The Esplanade
Toronto, Ontario
Canada   M5E 1R2

90 91 92 93 5 4 3 2 1

Introduction

I hate Andy Donato because he is a cartoonist. As a matter of fact, I hate all cartoonists. The reason I hate all cartoonists is because I envy them so. They have a licence a mere scribbler has not.

Let a columnist call a politician a poltroon, a cad, a blackguard, a charlatan and an intellectual pervert — publishers blanch, editors quake, weak-spined lawyers are called in — and what emerges is mere piffle. Donato can draw the same portrait and the bloke emerges quite clearly as a foul beast one would not let near the children, let alone the dogs and horses.

There is no limit to what a cartoonist can get away with. He is allowed to be twice as cruel as a columnist — and takes this advantage. If Fotheringham wrote his unflattering portrait in a column, the legal staff of the Toronto *Sun* would be able to afford yet another weekend in Ocho Rios. Not fair. Not fair at all.

The number of times the harmless columnist is hauled into the libel courts is proof of the unfairness. Words can be defined, analyzed, dissected and put under the microscope of the dictionary. There's no room in a column for freelance character assassination — the stock-in-trade for any self-respecting cartoonist. In Donato's case, it is red meat and strong drink to him, a man who gets genuine pleasure in the abattoir approach to editorial cartooning.

The scribbler is frequently seen in libel court, while it is rare to see an artist in those august chambers. In the one and only case within memory, Victoria's Bob Bierman was sued by Bill Vander Zalm. Bierman showed then-welfare minister Vander Zalm picking the wings off flies — with great glee. The judge rejected the ingenious defence lawyer's contention that in fact the politician was pasting the wings back on, but a sensible appeal court overturned the goofy decision and Vander Zalm, the only leader in the world who lives in a castle in a theme park, became another victim of the artist's pen.

It's all so unjust. When a columnist carves up a ripe target, he rushes to his lawyer. When Donato does it, the first thing his victim does is rush to the phone and ask for the original. There is no known case in history of a politician, stabbed by the truth, asking for a framed reprint of the column.

Donato is yet more proof that Canada — for its size — produces an inordinate proportion of world-standard cartoonists: Macpherson, Peterson, Aislin. He makes it look easy and laughs while he does it. I hate him.

Allan Fotheringham

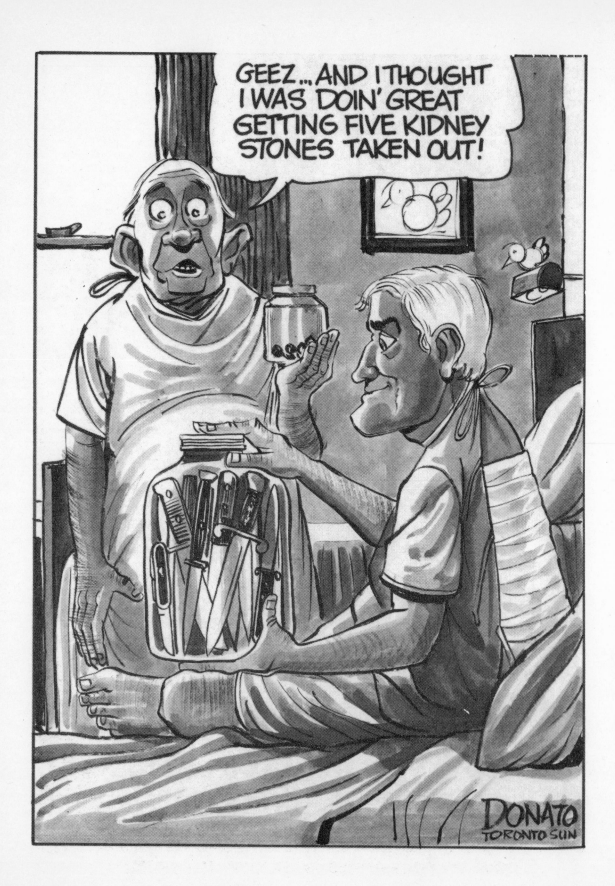

HOW TO FIND A $150,000 HOUSE IN TORONTO

LET'S SWARM 'IM!
MIKE THE SPIKE
FEDERAL SALES TAX
DONATO TORONTO SUN

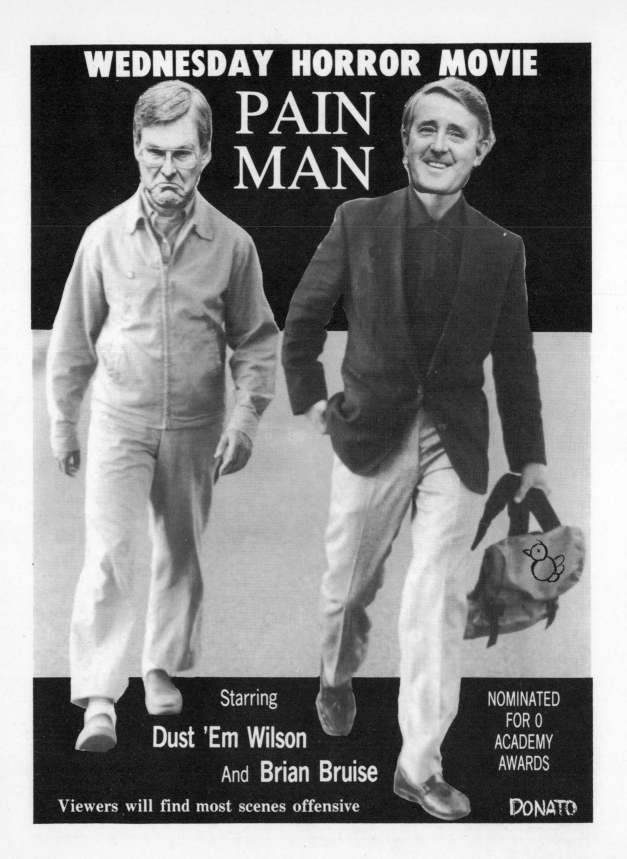

1986

1987

1988

1989

THE CHANGING FACE OF RUSSIA

QUEBEC
COURT
of APPEAL

DONATO *TORONTO SUN*

LOOK BRIAN... NO VELCRO!
THE House IS NOT A Home
by ERIK NIELSEN
DONATO
TORONTO SUN

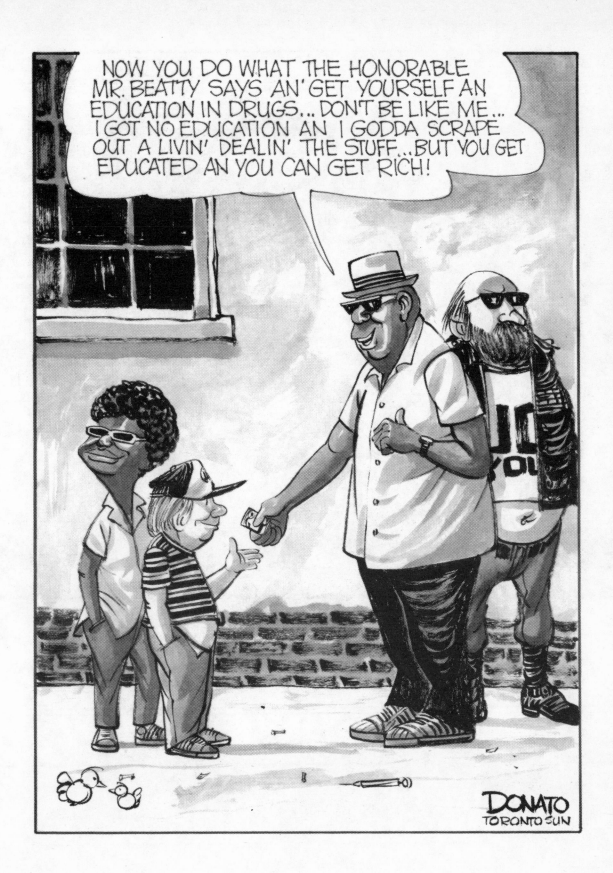

THE LAST SPIKE

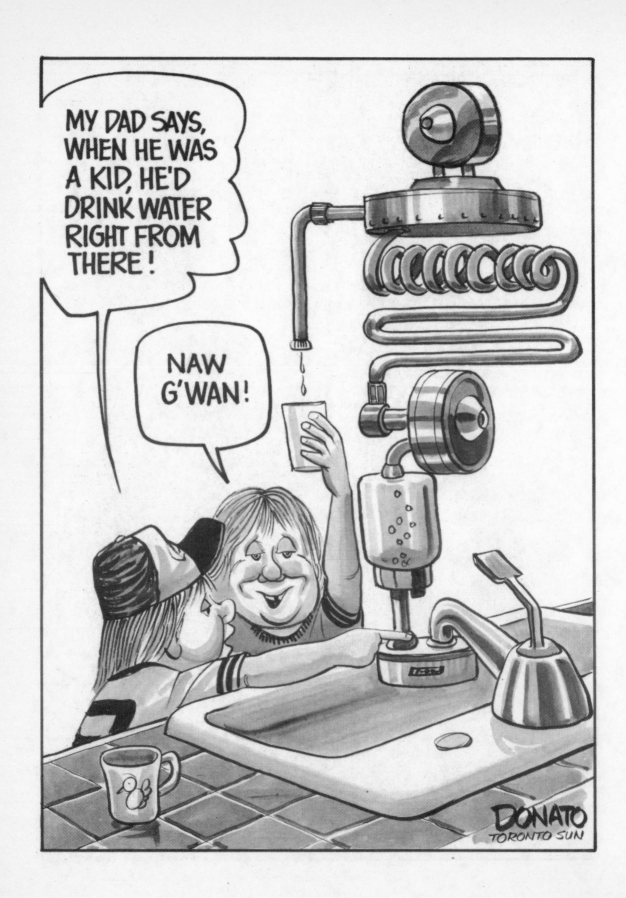

ONE, RAM IT...
ONE, SHOVE IT...
THREE, FORGET IT...
TWO, TRY AGAIN AND
THREE, NO WAY JOSÉ!
GST
PROVINCIAL
SUGGESTION
BOX
DONATO
TORONTO SUN

WONDERFUL SPEECH ON SANCTIONS, BRIAN... TAKE A BOW!
DONATO
TORONTO SUN

THE PREMIER OF MANITOBA SHOWS THAT A WATERED DOWN VERSION OF
THE *DISTINCT SOCIETY* CLAUSE IN THE MEECH LAKE ACCORD WOULD
BE MORE APPROPRIATE

DONATO *TORONTO SUN*

THE HONORABLE MEMBER FROM MISS**ASS**AUGA SOUTH

ONTARIO'S MOTHER

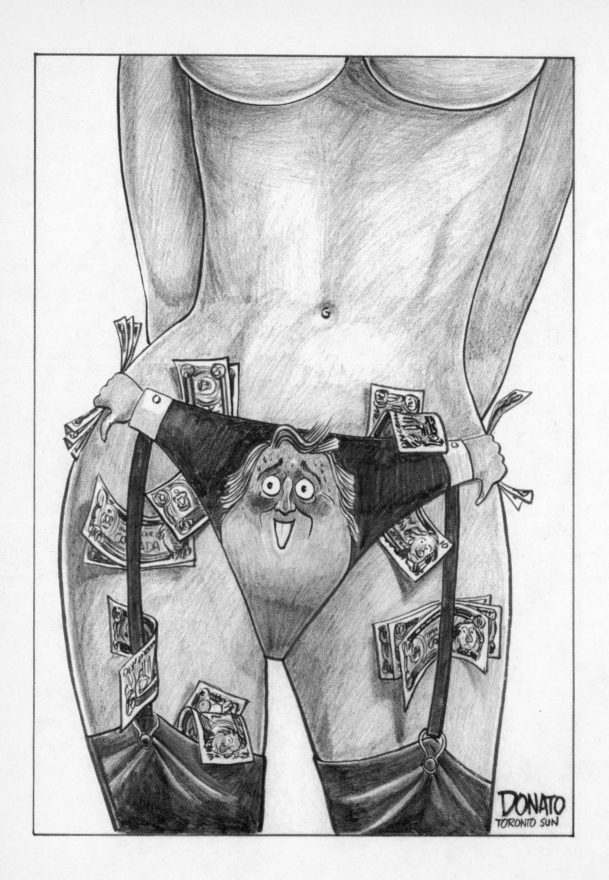

DONATO
TORONTO SUN

AND it came to pass in those days, that there went out a decree from Caesar Augustus, that all the world should be taxed.

2 (*And* this taxing was first made when Cȳ-rḗ-nĭ-ŭs was governor of Syria.)

3 And all went to be taxed, every one into his own city.

4 And Joseph also went up from Galilee, out of the city of Nazareth, into Judaea, unto the city of David, which is called Bethlehem; (because he was of the house and lineage of David:)

5 To be taxed with Mary his espoused wife, being great with child.

6 And so it was, that, while they were there, the days were accomplished that the tax rate was to be announced.

7 And, lo, the angel of the Lord came upon them, and the glory of the Lord shone round about them: and they were sore afraid.

8 And the angel said unto them, Fear not: for, behold, I bring you good tidings of great joy, which shall be to all people.

9 For unto you is born this day in the city of David a sales tax, not of 9% but 7%.

10 And suddenly there was with the angel a multitude of the heavenly host praising God, and saying,

11 Glory to God in the highest, and on earth, 7% good will toward men and retailers.

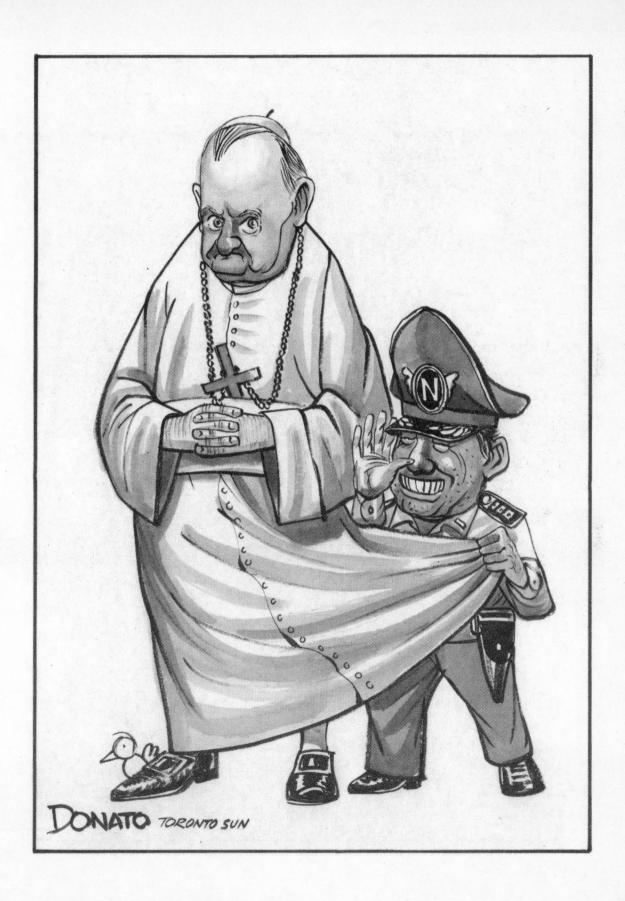

DONATO TORONTO SUN

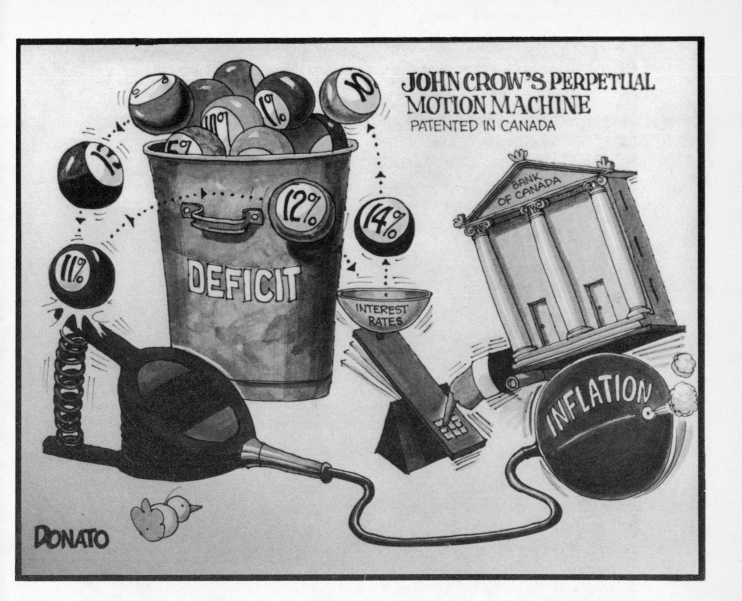

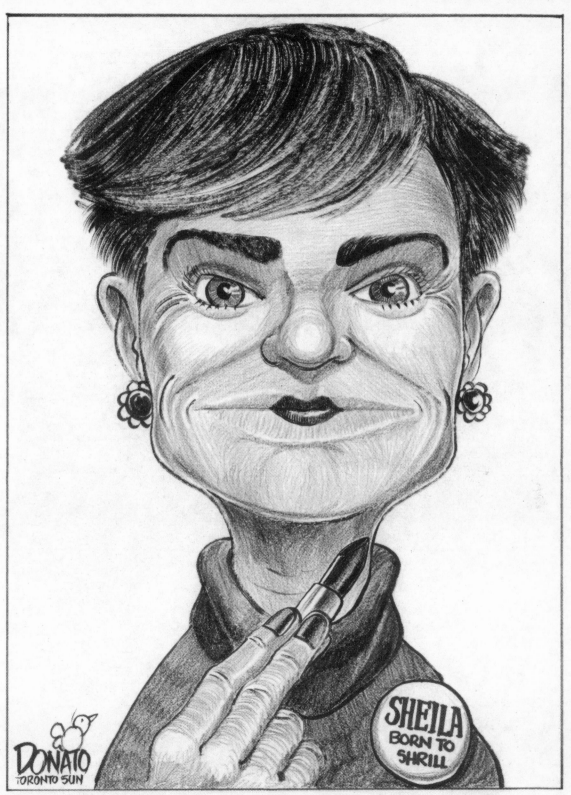

THE NEW IMAGE

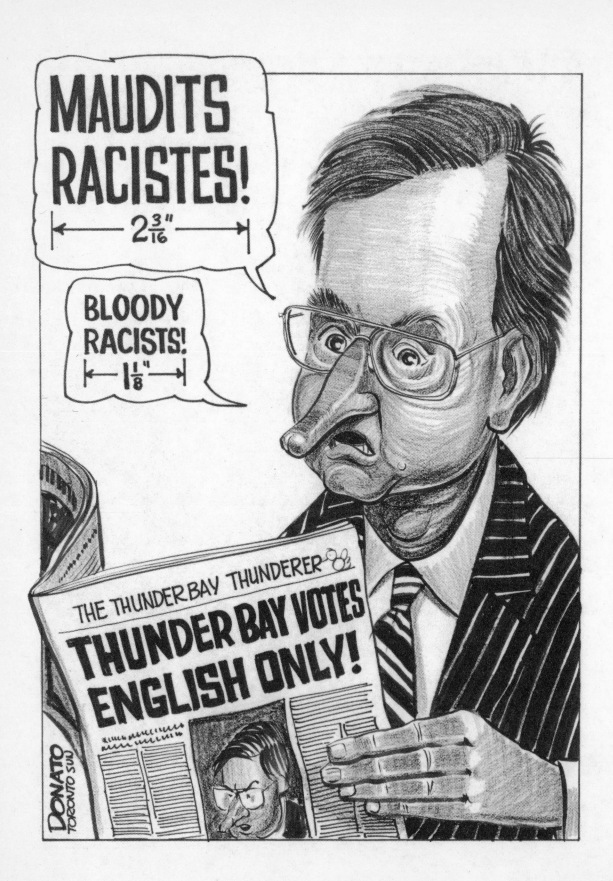

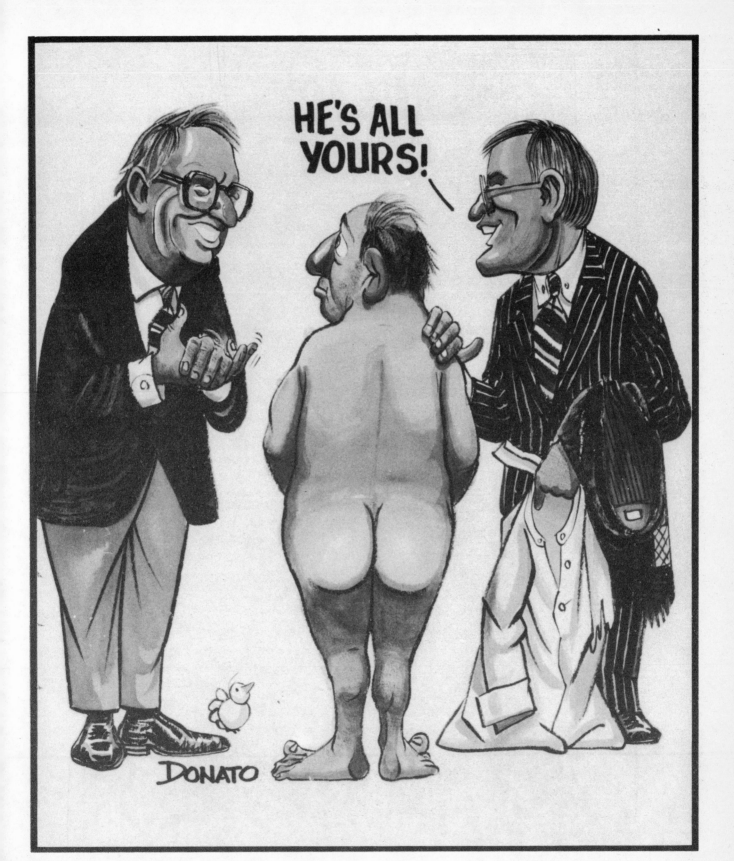

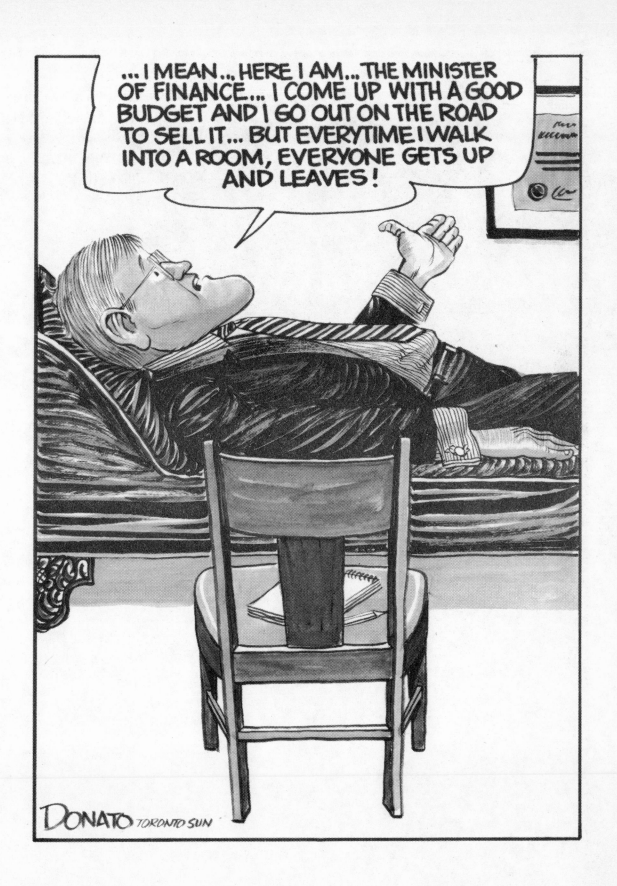

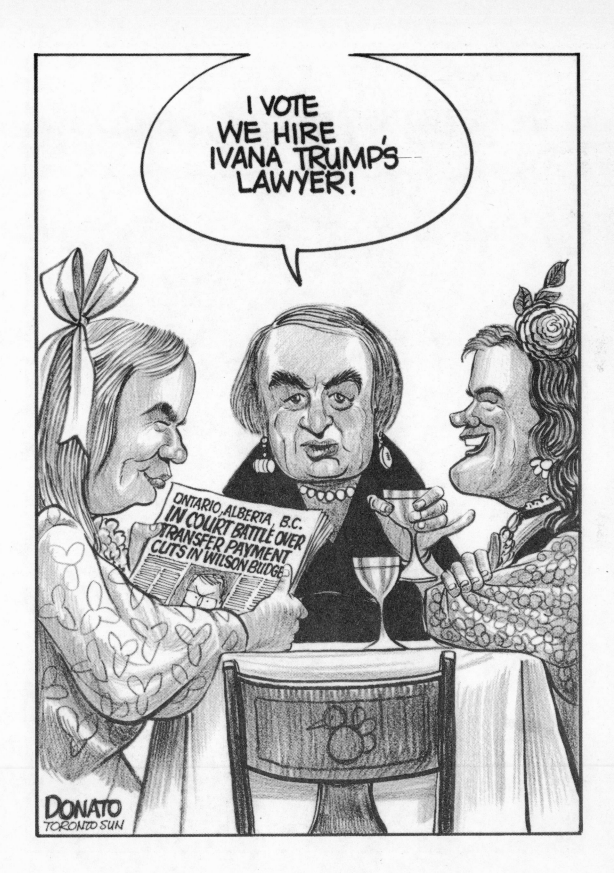

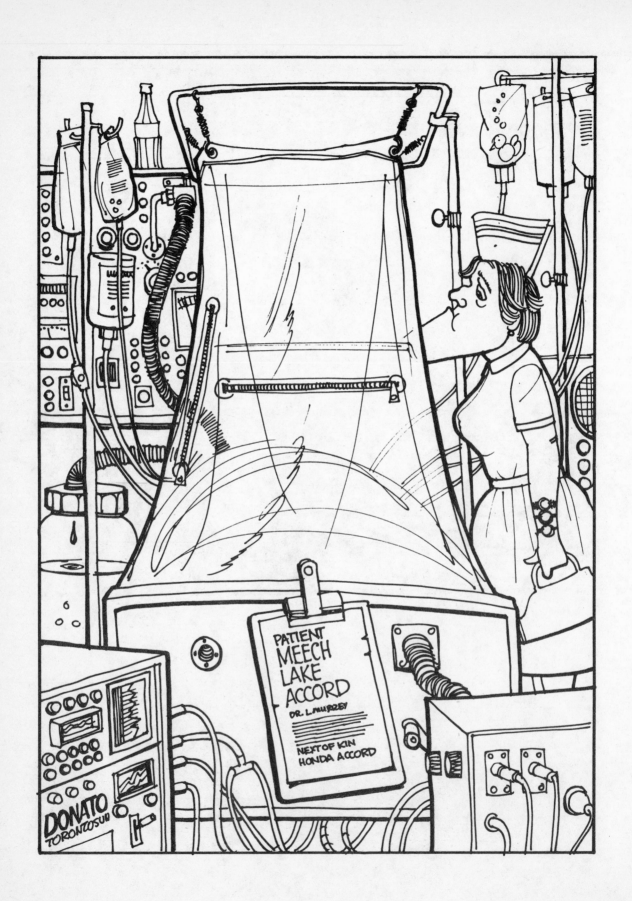

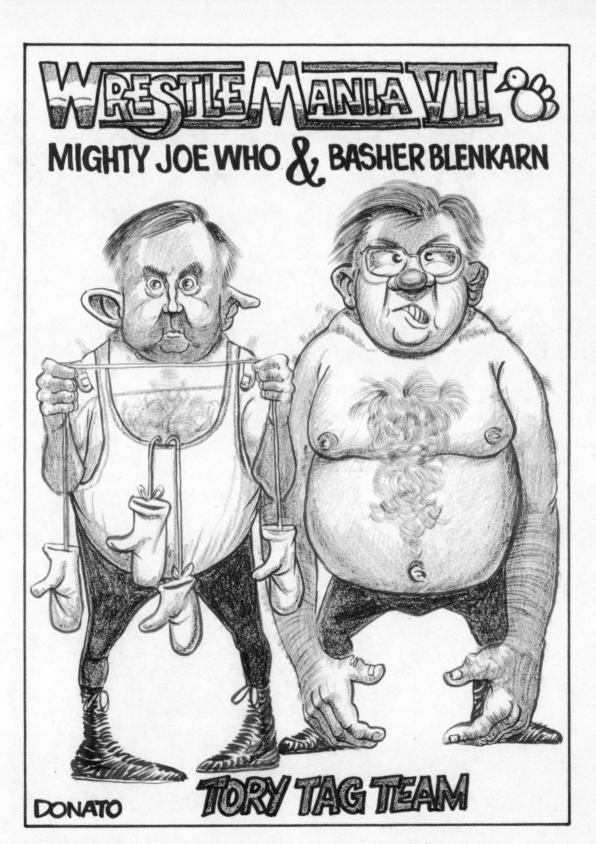

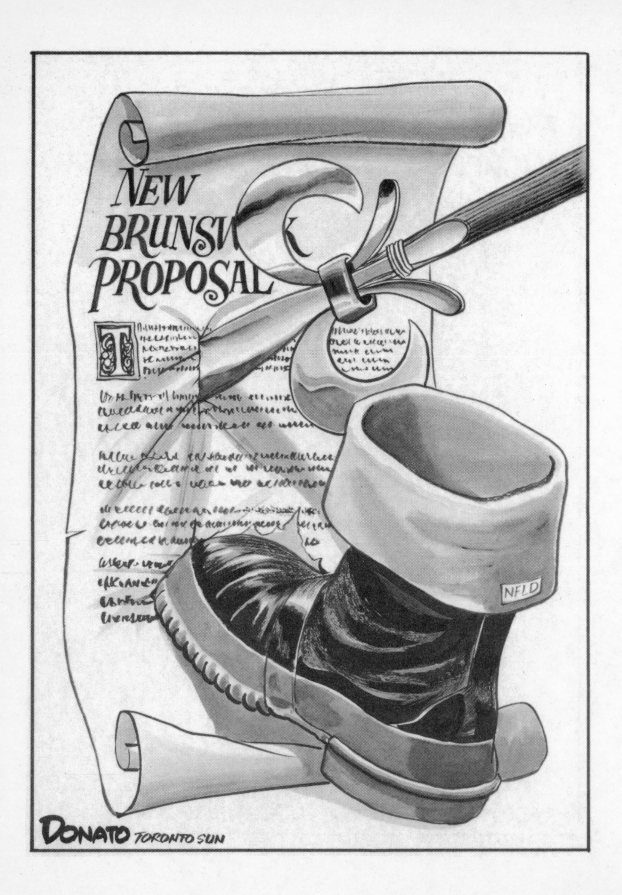

BEST ACTOR IN A POLITICAL ROLE

CROW'S NEST

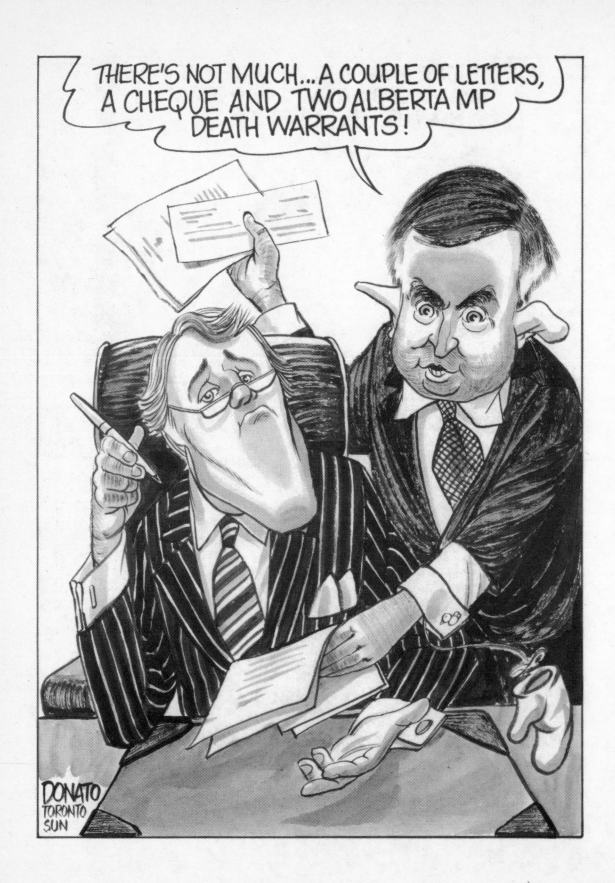

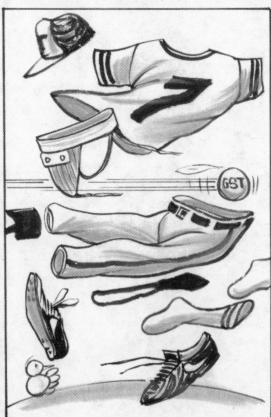

DONATO *TORONTO SUN*

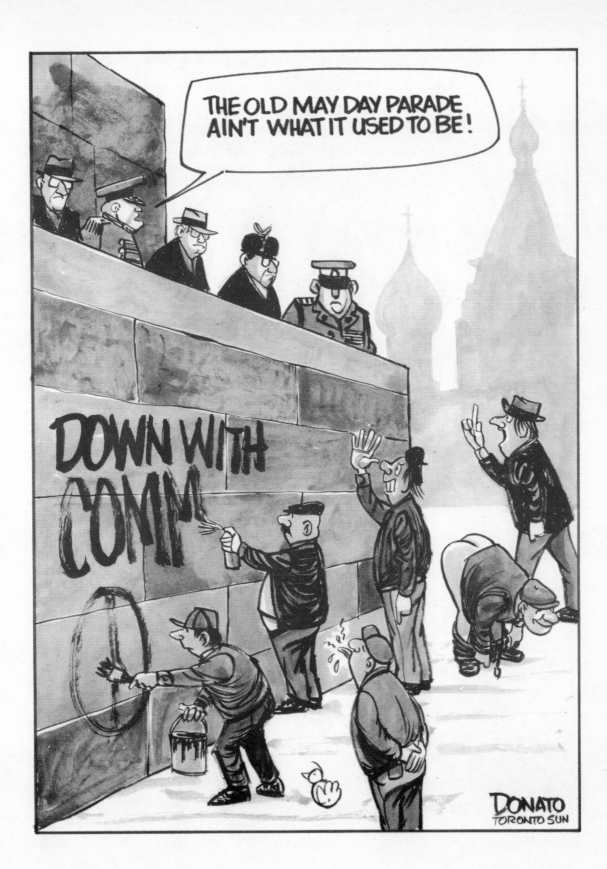

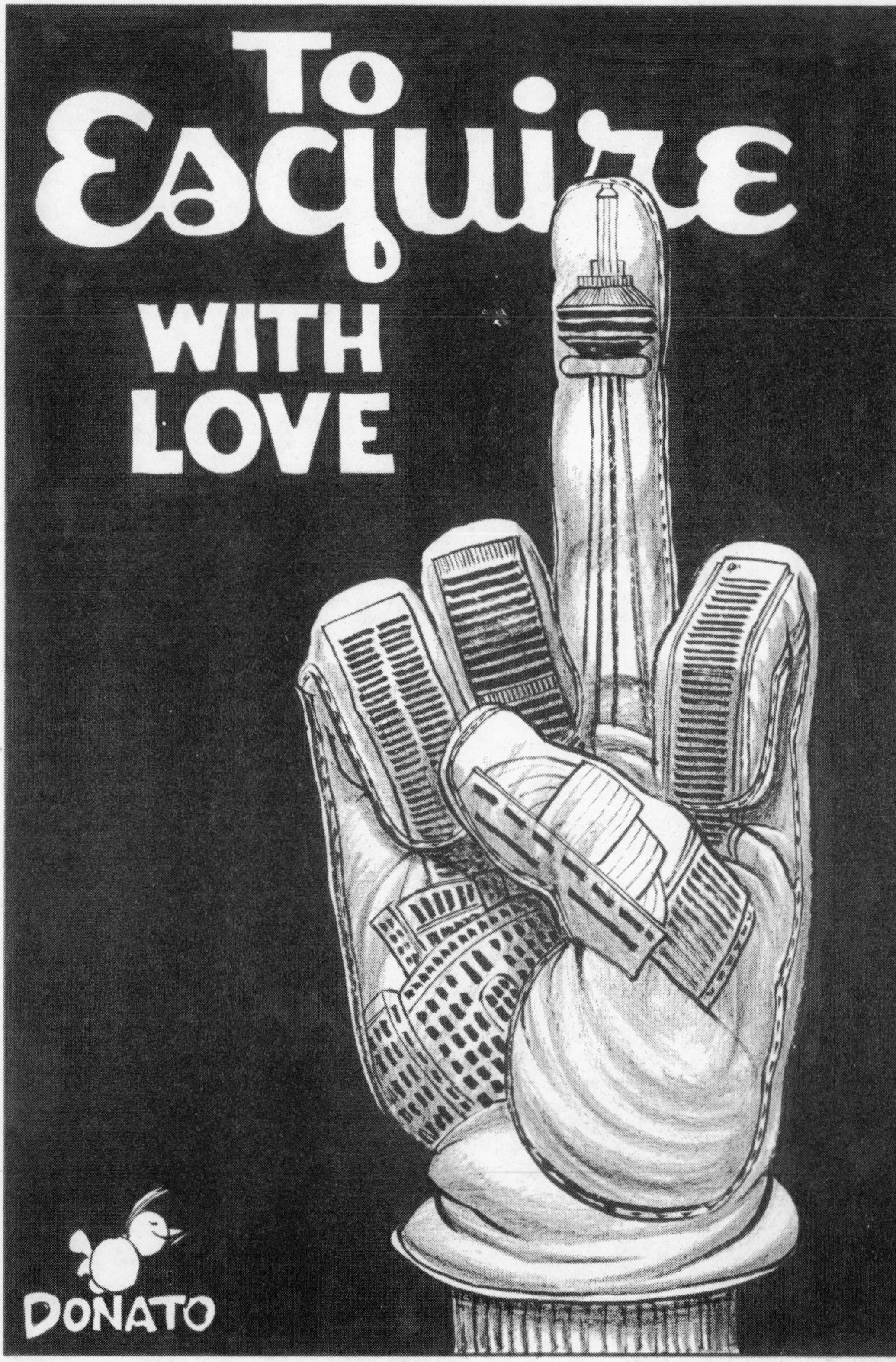
To
Esquire
WITH
LOVE
DONATO

24 SUSSEX

WE RECYCLE

DONATO *TORONTO SUN*

MINISTER OF THE ENVIRONMENT

IF YOU HAD TO PIN IT DOWN TO ONE THING, PRIME MINISTER, WHAT WAS IT THAT KILLED THE MEECH LAKE ACCORD?
DONATO
TORONTO SUN

A COURT

GOVERNMENT
OF
CANADA
VS
DOUGLAS
SMALL

DONATO *TORONTO SUN*

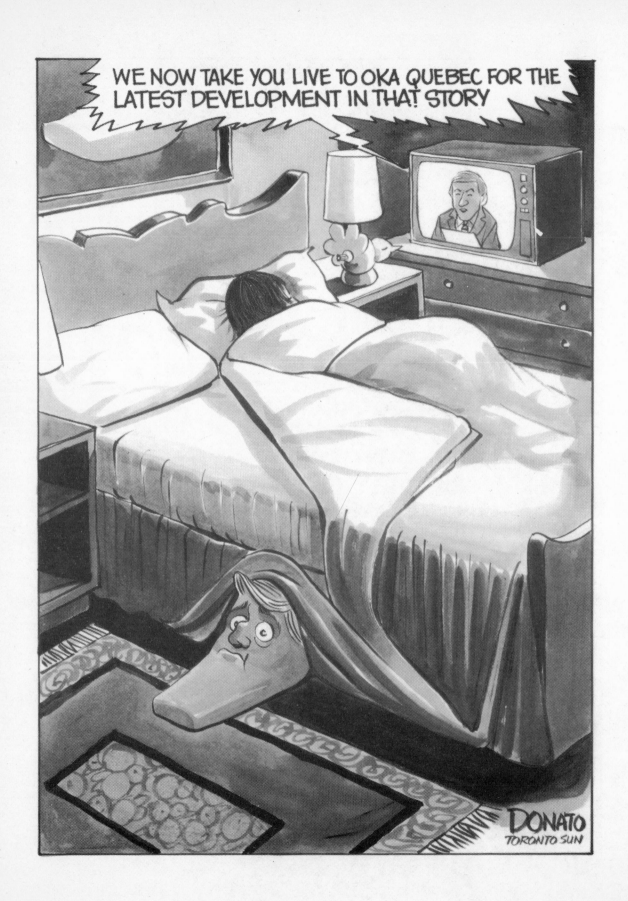